FOSSILS
IN THE MAKING

For Charles —
With gratitude for
your poetry!

April 2019
Ventura

Fossils in the Making

Kristin George Bagdanov

Black Ocean
Boston · Detroit · Chicago

Black Ocean
P.O. Box 52030
Boston, MA 02205
blackocean.org

Design by Nikkita Cohoon | nikkita.co

ISBN 978-1-939568-28-1

A CIP record is on file with the Library of Congress.

FIRST EDITION

For Levi

CONTENTS

PROOFS

WAGERS

REMAINS

In every part of every living thing
is stuff that once was rock

In blood the minerals
of the rock

— Lorine Niedecker, "Lake Superior"

Contain is what a body does
Until it doesn't and spills itself
        "Contain"

Contain *is what a body does*
Until it doesn't then spells itself.
        "Of the Vegetative Night"

—Bin Ramke, *Missing the Moon*

Lines Written After Crisis

The privilege of having / to imagine // of can't even imagining
The dream of children but also the fear
That nothing is / disposable because nothing can be
Our gyre / widens wider now it is plastic
Oracle that reads / in glowing teeth a future now // past
Orpheus singing into the ears of leaves / a song to re / wind eternity
As aphids conscripted to protect & serve / the surplus
After the emergency / resolution in bullet // points
As if speech were a carcass / mounted upon a wall
Were your caress a revolution that could // make a tyrant fall
When bodycam mediation / mediates no justice
West Coast waking up // crisis always in medias res
After the planes hit / the teacher told the class this was their war
And mourning would make a method // to take / from every / form

PROOFS

Proof of Harm

This one measures tidal flux against plastic gyre
            crest against breast   of least tern   brown pelican
            more brown now but also more red and yellow
                                    the slick turned rainbow
            the bow of the boat nuzzles against the soft
                                    floating bodies in animal fashion
            in which nose is more trustworthy than hand
            in which scent alerts hair and skin   index of harm or help
                                                contiguous
            but not synonymous with language which could be called reason

This one measures the speed of sound against the body
            when one person calls for help
            vs. another
            when one is told to raise their hands
            when one is asked to raise their hand and is called on
            and asked to answer
            vs. told to answer for
            their body

This one measures those two knocking against each other
            crest against breast as one person least brown calls for help
            another person is told to raise their hands more
            brown more red the sick turning
            toward the bow raised against the soft bodies

as one asks which is more trustworthy and scent alerts skin
that is contiguous with language
and synonymous with sound
of bodies knocking against the hull

Prey

When an animal catches its prey
when I'm caught I pray to all the bodies
decomposing who cry   *touch me*
once more   Every body frustrates desire
by loving what's outside its skin
When my lord touches his body   its harness
as he lays   saying   being said
a thousand ears stoop unto ground
for the great articulation   He answers
in lightning and they descend
into their stooping and my lord strikes
and his body makes mine stand up
on end   illuminates its bulk
my life becomes the anticipation of
my body   shudders against
its limit   to becompose

Corpus

If my body is an illness, then my bones
are a tangle of sea trash, plastic six-pack
that chokes the bottlenose. And if migration

to eternity is ocean weed beached in clumps
that dissolves in mouthfuls of fly vomit

                then

                        the cure is a blade that severs
                        mussel from shell as well
                        as hand, hand split
                        beneath the shell
                        its blood in the water, the dark
                        shape that tastes it.

Proof of Parasite

Geometry compels conclusion   as when an orchid's stamen girth

       & petal edge comports the male's thorax rhythm a coming

predicted by Euclid, codified by Darwin   deception of sex

       the first cause of evolution   of wasp warping at the mouth

          of *Ophrys speculum*

Inside a caterpillar's belly the female wasp buries her eggs:

        the unsuspecting surrogate performs

        spinning & mouth clenching & leaf cutting

        Ready for transformation, it stretches

        toward the chrysalis

        & turns host instead

        Larvae hungry to unfold themselves

ride the holey body till their wings hold

Glistening with saliva, the green sheath

collapses with their absence

Cf: how the female wasp replaces another's eggs with her own:

labor can be exploited even in nature

even in nature many do not want to be mothers

So the eggs grow under another mater   no matter

Who could know their eggs from another's?

Imagine the sterile line-up   the police line-up

of bodies wet & glistening & no smell

to smell yourself home   Who would know

their own phylum class family species   genealogies

that say you belong

as if everything were non-undulating & not inside an other always

　　　　already unfolding in the other

　　　　It is impossible to prove　　impossible

　　　　to measure the distance between membrane & mother

　　　　circulation of cells that makes a self of what enters

　　　　your mouth

So you spin a skin around you

　　　　as if you were more than the sum of your parts

　　　　as if you were more than what's becoming

　　　　inside & through you & you become

　　　　in their mouths

　　　　what you never were

　　　　yourself

Calving

creature of our own breaking

       each body
       a velocity
       silent ache inside
       the ice crystal

: structure of intimacy :

       we never notice
       subaerial melting
       the slow wedge   until

I am   : & :   you are

       each birth an absence
       chiseled
       from the old

sinking form   : :   stillborn

Earth

                    break
Two plates will   into mountain
                    grind

measure their reach in millennia

          soul
So my   verb not noun not now but always
          self

                    wool   chews
chafes my body: that
                    will   moves

          passing without
          passing by

A year of silence: I

               thinking   body
thought my   was my
               flesh   fear

O

    guttural

    lurch: continental drift   the inch

        each shifts: I am

strangers once more

        world
    This is the   that ends in inches
        self
that regards the   and cringes
      body

Proof of Extension

I express the shape of clouds   but not their substance
            which is heavy yet diffuse   I think
inside the lonely cloud and the wandering one too
            as they think in me   Diaphanous composing
                        change then stay then *was*

            I was a knowing thing   I trusted my body
the apparatus of truth   Don't say such things
            and expect anyone to believe you
says my body   Don't say, just think

through the quiet death and regeneration of mitochondria
through the calculus of glucose that roots for our survival
through the million billion parts that do not make a whole
            that do but do not produce the sum of this body

A rigorous thought is a cloud   Do not trust its color
            Refraction of light in ash made London beautiful once
made smoke divine   particle gods radiating faces of people
who perhaps believed in space   without thinking

This mind   is only lonely because it is thinking itself

        out of existence   dissipating without trace

                cloud reaching toward   its own embrace

Wander

I wandered thoughtlessly

I wondered at a face
reflected in shallows

I understood nothing
but surface

My arm reached inside
and disappeared

My hand
would not show me
what it saw

only gave me
its reaching

A fly is important

The surface said

A fly is important

The depth allowed

Trebled noise: wing tips abuzz with wind's own voice
hear the hollow   hear it offer its mouth to us all

Wake

give me any lyre-like thing

I'm on my knees

        what

I'm on my knees

*

the swamp I move
through

        careful

your own drowning
is at hand

*

presume breath &
you will always be
disappointed

presume death
& be
a hand reaching

*

counting backwards
from nothing

wake me

                    Lord

the waiting
take that too

Proof of Thought

Before the shelf holds
Before the screw threads
Before the head turns
Before the open / closed hand
sounds the stud
Before breath condenses
this eggshell structure of mind

You, human, remember
this gap
divides you

this *thing*
we call me and mine.

Lord

when the lord says *thank you* he means *you take*

when the lord makes a miracle he means *you under-*
mothered child of exile

when the lord touches his selves they say *shudder, world*
with me

my body came free but its balance stays—
two feet, two ears, a queer sound
in my throat: *echo, world, in me*

everything starts as free until matter
makes a demand: *live in it, bite this lip, batter my face*
O *three-dimensional god*

and now the air is thicker
but also more distant

I see a horizon:
what makes & exceeds it:

there is a cloud glowing
there is a child growing

we will feed it
this world

Proof of Hunger

I feed my body less and want more   the surplus
I was promised   storehouses of grain   plains of locust
don't signify a thing without hunger
telos that defers its own ending

          Which isn't to say I've a vision

or can calculate a head of grain against a golden calf
in a crisis or pinch or hitch in which a child   (there is always a child)
born tomorrow judges me for my lack
of discretion, brings legal action against my hunger
which wouldn't have existed were it not for the child's face
always looming before me   asking me to materialize
          what won't

I stock my dreams like cans in a bunker   I wait
for doom   siphoning off a day here and there   I store the future
in a sack with a hole through which a mouse lives and dies happy
I eat its shit knowingly and with envy of its tiny gut

          Which isn't to say I've promised anything

only that I've considered the balance   I weighed the future
against my hunger and found it   wanting   found the surplus was only
my own body working twice as hard then harder   hardening itself
against a future I had already consumed

Flesh

So long since
I have tasted
blood : animal
in my animal

composing body.

Corn&soybean
chain-of-being my
bodymind mine but
not my own. Share
this crop with no one,
no thing? *To have*

someone growing inside you, you can't even imagine.
Yesyes I can: all the mothers
mothering me without consent. Yes
I know the feeling of being
consumed from the inside
out. Mouthful of flesh
I speak through, through which:
this being.

Mother

My mother was a body
       of water. Her water

body mothered me
       my sack of cells stretching.

My father was an organ donor
       organ grinder: sound

churned whole. Hear the mechanism
       rumble, how water makes it

       rust.

       My mother body and my
       father body shake hands
       outside my sack of body
       to model how a truce is
       made, the exchange of my
       baby body a dotted line on
       a numbered page.

Swallow

Blue heron on the bank
        purple gradient of wing
strained neck to pluck a fish
        from the stream.

What is it like
        to see that great shadow hovering
above? I'm trying not to
        make this a metaphor
            but I have to
        ask which I would be: fish
or bird, the water, the dam?

        The heron swallows
    a sleek length of trout and I
imagine it convulsing like jonah
        inside the whale except
            there is another metaphor
and now I am asking god how he calls
        the fish food and not the man and I am asking
            again what I am—
fish or bird or man?
All of them convulsing,
        each inside the other?

Song

Moon made
by what gets in the way

sun that makes
it so
makes it dark

enough for world
bright enough
to pull

*

God ungiving
        voice that spoke:
                echo of night
                                in
                        gale

Grieve with me: still
bird   still now:
we only wanted you so
we could hold song
in our hands

*

All words are song
if we hold them gently
inside
our mouths

even the wolf
carries her young
without puncture

even the moon
has sphere
and so
a song

Word

      after Paul Celan

They did not grow wise   *invented no song*
song: a sound we made   when tongue was a made thing
thing: a gesture we drew   in mud   muscle we grew
into mind

         we're never given the chance to sacrifice
         to carve *love* with a blade that reaches
         eternity, to carve with tongue a new
         yearning

What becomes of song   once it leaves the body?
It reveals every   eye every open mouth and
pore: pouring   like water into world

         when *the* was still and *song* was
         silence   when *word* was
         only what was: what was only

a broken   broken glass:
it reflects this blood   mouth, blood melody

            of tongue   its song
            my only sacrifice
            my every

Proof of Infinity

the feedback loop of wound winding from father to son to spouse to stranger
        bad infinity no different than good, only potential   as in

each of our bodies is source and citation etching a future through the past
        as when one person makes history by killing the others

or when one person makes earth by remattering one's body, which can't be
        erased, only dispersed: infinite loop of decomp & comp

as when an arrangement of mirrors tries to disappear a face but only splits it
        more finely, the being becoming smaller & smaller
            but not the distortion of being

no meeting or meaning to come of it all after all   asymptotic always
        nearer but never *here*   the heaping & piling up of numbers
            which are bodies & bodies which are numbers

we approach apocalypse without arriving futile in a future too deep
        to be filled   as in   we are always a part of and apart
            from time no matter the stacking of words on end

the line snaking toward infinity that bites its own tail after all   as in
        the comfort is there is possibility the violence is there is plenty

Wound

Thoreau's the rose of his own wood, his own
body,　　　　how nice to sit inside a wood of your own

no baby there to test it, interjecting
its small fact, itself sounding <i> until it becomes a

me / myself　　　　　　that / who can refer to its
as "itself" / "myself"　　　the choice

to live deeply　to suck the　bone
could be mine　　if only　　 had a wood in which

could escape　these disobedient　ovaries, too many possible
selves　wish they would stack　nice & clean:

woodpile　　fuel for myself　But the <i> is sublime
in the wood　　　　he says only listen and men will, will
disobey their father bodies　　　　to hunt their animal bodies

 should go watch their selves' animal bodies' heads
turn　　to this inaudible pitch:　　the moon
scream　　　　inside me　　　clean

shot　　through their eyes, the wound <i> touch
 bloody myself,　　my i

Harvest

Howl at the moon body don't
be late for school body
you won't fool any body
when your fingers swell in heat.

A man harvests his
life   clean scythe
while the woman waits
                    to be winnowed.

How quaint. Our shells
of selves   propped
on shelves   stuffed
with tissue   from birth

days past: creased then saved
for a future
for ankles that won't swell
in the heat

              of bodies of every
body's furrowed-brow
fear chuffed under
their skins: this sweltered
pelt   this plasma self   my final
birthday
          body

Proof of Sorrow

a tree felled in a forest takes the length of its life to return to

                                         a tree felled in the equation of

soil & I wonder about the equation for sorrow

                                         sorrow where x equals a line

whether it can be split and stacked

                                         planted in the nest of decay

with such clean symmetry where *x* equals *y*

                                         a tree felled in the nest of decay

a line plotted in the matrix

                                         the line that draws an infinite slope

of decay

Code

Coughing blood—one tooth, another. Canine
       or molar doesn't matter when all you eat

is water, some broth. I curdled milk
       for cheese, squeezed a lemon with my fist.

I pump your hand with language, a code
       that tells your heart its time.

How can grass know it will be milk?
       Or churned harder, a wet slab of butter?

If I were another man I would have smothered you
       in that richness, smeared your sores with fat.

Heart greased, your valve might have opened,
       slid past its sickness and answered

Making

Mouth full of dirt

Swallow: a gesture that reaches toward

That I made mud with my voice

Wandering tongue

God forgive

O dark lung

I work from memory of when I had begun

When first I heard my self give birth

WAGERS

See the sea as
hollow : filled

by the great accumulation

My cells accumulate their selves
and others

                    atomic trace in my teeth
                    which I pull to bury

                    proof of existence or
                    stratigraphic strategy

I asked for another body
once   Once I was

               given a stone

I asked for another
and asked for another

                    Fill my hollow,
                    lithic lover

It is a choice:

      the view from the sea / island

are you habiting or inhabiting:

      the question that curates being

a record

      of what saw me / my body

            before / after the great accumulation

the sea / island cannot exist without

      a world / body that experiences

            its island / sea as a body / world

What is before:

      the leaving or the rooting?

            And how does a migration begin and who makes it so?

      cell   glucose   antibody   babybody

Make the body hollow:

      room for the not-body but not the anti-body

I asked for another body once
Once I was given a stone

and asked
to hallow :

I asked
to follow :

I asked
for another

Once I was
given a stone

then another
and an other

building
what a body leaves:

(in)visible record
of what we want

to see see
sea island sea

I asked for another body once.

       Once I was given a stone and asked to hollow :

I incorporate this ache of granite

my chest tightens around it, learns to live with the condition

love it, maybe   unconditional until I am crowded

out by smaller bodies   cell glucose antibody babybody

      I asked for another body once.

         Once I was given a stone and asked to follow :

all day my babybody decays all day my body leans into a shadow that

      runs away

         (once I brushed my fingers against it,

         the shadow)

I asked for another body once.

         Once I was given a stone and asked to hallow :

before touch and its residue fades

        less than a minute for a body to circulate its blood

always rising to the surface of skin

        the condition of being at rest or in motion

of needing a mouth that leaves

        the mark of its own hollow

the condition of a warm body

        : to make its limit

Love   it leans into stone

I asked for a body
to decay all bodies   cell   glucose   world

a warm body I once touched

we sense
our condition
this family system

we sense the sky is no limit

touch it, maybe
unconditional until
                                    I'm given a stone
and asked...

the condition of needing
of being at rest or in motion

              love
              it learns to live
              in the rooting

I hear my animal body shedding : I cannot stay a thing

We are a family system   a system of jaguars leopard monkey lepers

In the darkness we touch our animal bodies
      repeatedly we try to breach our limits
We will die trying: peeling back the layers of body
      trying to hear what else there is

      I hear my animal body chewing : I cannot taste a thing

When an animal catches its prey I pray to all the bodies
decomposing. When we are risen again when we walk across
the field of bones let me recompose let me take whale's jawbone
baby's kneecap. Let me becompose

      I hear my animal body burning : I cannot say a thing

Once I was given a stone and
a warm body

incorporate them, maybe
a stone body

      Once I tried to empty my bones

but the world
hinges on cell glucose antibody

      wound and limit.

When we walk across our limit
when we touch it
will *should/would have* still exist?

Once I tried to empty my body I tried to dig out the river inside me but the digging made the river wider made a deep rut in my gut.

Beneath this surface air for one only

the smaller bodies nest inside me, waiting

they do not know what is dark and what is light

what is you and what is I

So I filled my body up with sand and the small skeletal bodies of mice and other creatures like an owl, following the beaked wisdom, but that too proved a mistake. My body would not hold what I had asked— neither would it let it go.

Every moon cycle breaks my body open

the wound a perfume for the dead

bodies who wish their bodies would still wound

When I die where will my body go

where will the oil flow

will it become a new body

will it peat into coal

will my body be fuel for other bodies

will it shine bright like the moon before the earth made it small?

I hear bodies in migration
circulation & accumulation
the ache of others

body be body but what else is there?

Once I was given again what
I tried to want.
Once I tried
to want to die

I filled my bones with this
worldache &
oilflow
I waded out in the lake
but it would not take

god:

I am turned outside-in

love:

it learns to live *with*

we
How could   know?
I

REMAINS

cause / effect

My body wants   to see inside itself   it listens
        for the symptoms of its making   the small labors of digestion
& disintegration   unradical until I try to draw a line between
        crust & cuticle   me & not-quite-me

Once, one cell became, became two : two
cells emerged together in their making
neither first nor second   neither second nor first
       just (un)split   just call call call
     no need for response   no need for it
       echo hinged to the voice like shadow

Sound is a matter I can't dissect   I trace the mouths
of faces on the screen
            saying *goodbye*
            saying *I will die*
            throats full of unthought things:
                 loves unspoke
                 & songs to sing

No nightingale left

to carry voice upon wing

Wholeness isn't all I thought it would be:

leave a little room

(please)

between cause & effect

me & not-yet-me

the speech that makes death

and the dead

sediment / sentient

What is body without a wager
without a pressure to coal
the peat, to squeeze its wager
of water

a burial which without a world is null.

My body / wager shifts and dips
inside itself: loon on a glacial lake
that evaporates
around it.

Loon in a pond loon in a puddle of sediment

sentience is the wager
we all bet
we forget

our value, the commodity body
we must share we must
lock, stock
& bury.

future / past

when today was still the future of the past
when many saw their lives extending into it

> like one arm with many hands
> each one waving a flag
> on which was written
> the adage of our age:
> reach for courage
> and find rage

Time the first
betrayer, yes:

> Orpheus wrapping himself
> in tree limbs each night
> singing into the ears of leaves

> to re-
> wind
> eternity

The only moment that matters
is the one when you look back
into newly conjured absence
the trace of one possible future a mist
in which no angel waits
to gather the accidents of history

when the turn was still the future
around which everything might

gyres widen wider now they are plastic
chains of polystyrene guard the absence at the center

$(C_8H_8)_n$ the gravesite and gravemarker of a future
that bonds with tide-moon-gravity
as with birdbeak-fishbelly-breastmilk:

CH-TMG-BBFBBM

a new adage to outlast
the holy chanting
of vowelled breath

sacrifice / circumference

I entered this world without looking
without needing to look
at me pale as paper
some hands
make bowls
the depth of longing
for enough meat to fill
the strange beast living in the sacrifice
zone & another
I've been made
aware of
without
needing to be in
side its circumference
outside there is a mouth always listen
ed to, weight of a body
never pressed
into
service
this proves no
thing but the logic
already embedded inside the dead
from which grow the living
mineral heart flinting
a spark

to mean
anything others
have told me have wanted me
to look where I was / we were going
but I never had to could
shut my eyes could let
papers burn
ash nothing
but proof that violence is
rational that I keep living
because someone else does not

memory / mattering

Memory of field grew also
         the memory of wire
barbed with fur

marks the crossing or
         hair, clump or tuft
the difference between me
         as the object of I and
                  I am

a field without memory of beneath be
         comes a surface on which roots
make branches out of nothing but
         air shared between our

haunches wound the fence or
         the other way around.
A field divides

membrane from mother, which is
         the labor of soil. Of what energy
mares the air. Membering the field a bound
         ary by which every
                  thing must

surface, the being *in* a breath
       less heat rising from
dirt, animal still
       yet to be named.

animal / flesh

In the beginning was the word, was the
breath that shaped it, mouth
that cupped the breath and the body
that made it. I am merely flesh, remaking

myself every seven years. I breathe to escape
my origin, caressing the unseen syllables
like rings of smoke that open
to dissolve. Trust me, you will

always be alone. We will always be separate in time:
the distance between   our bodies in bed
the distance between   your death and mine.

We come together at night to pretend
loneliness is an animal we can cull. I
watch you sleep, hair splayed across your pillow,
slack mouth breathing for your singular life.

soul / vestigial

In sleep the body mends itself, amends
the day, the pressure of light and how it bends
without rest to reach its object. Small crack
        in the door, green flare of the charger: no darkness
        no place left wholly its own.

Eyelids flutter like wings on the mayfly, *éphémère*:
shutter the morning, light that whelms the membrane,
vestigial windows to what might outlast a body
        and how it aches to utter in darkness, to hear
        its echo, residue of absence:

heart / here

It will stop it has
before when it was
notyet when it was
undulating plasma in coll-
apse when the friction of
chaos rubbed its flint its pulse
weak in all that notyetdark and
notyetlight: bleat of a wet lamb
notyetlicked not ever licked
clean it will make its own
way in this universe in every
universe its starheart
will beat eternally listen-
ing for a rhythm
that sounds
here.

slope / shell

No one knows what it's like to die,
to be unfeeling, to unspeak a life.

God himself has tried
to swallow back earth
and sky, the billions who
tumbled from his lips.

Here the unmended mender
rips open the mantle.
Into the tear trips anything that's felt.

Peak of a mountain—can it feel
its own base shake? Plumb line
to earth's core, vein bisects its middle.

Here is my slope, faulted
Here is my snow, melting

      for you
      for you

Take and slide
out from your body:

      calf from cow
      yolk from shell.

I will not wait to hear from you.
I will call your name until it is a stranger
at my ear. At my ear its echo
just another word for fear.

bleat / bleed

I am the weakest lamb.
I am the bleating
I am the bleeding

residue of what world
will soon be.

What use are the meek?
Their words cannot dull a blade,
unsplit sinew from bone.

Cannot uncast the stone
or hold a body's tears
with their unmarked faces.

Pasture me—splayed
hoof, lynx jaw, clover chewed to root—and I
might bleed into being.

I examine my own body
like a butcher: a pound
of this flesh
will bring no

great price.

monster / demonstrate

Plunge deep into socket: my memory

is gelatin   a mold of your face   only

blink and you will   quiver   my body my

    being made new

in your image   a shape

  like yours   eyes transparent

as language   a gaze that binds

    Tender this   monsterheart

with goat's milk   draw out

what is   wild   I drink

the dregs   wholly

    Churn my residue

into what can be seen.

I open my eyes:

    clovenhoof

   in the dirt I

  can't make clean

poem / field

The poem I am
writing is not a field
in which I find
or do not find my
self. There is no filling
of graves with dirt, no trans-
posing of blood and earth.
I do not give unto space
my absence, nor extract
my verse until a shadow
is coerced to speak also
my name. I cannot ask
you to watch me pleasure
this edge, either. The meeting
of tall grass with taller trees
a formula I am told bears
life, bares death where
coyote stalk and leave
a record of encounter:
two patches of fur snagged
on sagebrush. I cannot keep telling you
how frontier rhymes with fear
but not tear, as in, jaws
locked in an embrace uncovered
10,000 years from now, teeth
still sharp enough to draw

whatever blood becomes. Ten
thousand years, which I am told
is the limit of responsibility
of being able to respond to an
other looking back and asking
in the symbols of their making
why we could not contain what
we shed, the content oozing
out our vessels, decomposing steel
plated sarcophagi with patient address.
This poem wants to be
good, to mark on the map
the verve of making, to hold
your face in its jaws without puncture
the way coyote carry their young
against imminent darkness
which I am told will be thick as ash
and sweet as the cloud of white
churning behind trucks that dust
the crops at dusk, children shrieking
with delight as they chase the rest
of their lives that feeling of opening
their mouths to anything without
caring the source without knowing
the shape it will take inside
of breathing deep no matter
the matter it makes, the hunger
it will never sate.

tree / trace

Stand here long enough: reed in wind

       cupped hands
       & empty: a nest
       in winter

Spool a self inside a body

       Release it
       in inches like shadow
       like a gull that tests

its wings on cliffs at dawn on the day of your birth

       when water will betray
       its trace
       until water is also a trace

Close your eyes and a season will pass before you

       had you the century's gaze
       of a coast live oak

It will not survive this, either

It sheds bark
breaks branch

Lovers' carved symbols seeping their wound of sap

pulp / pulse

She tired of how a warm breeze
      unsettles a mood. The pain

of ripeness, the peach always ending
      in pit. An eternity of flesh that keeps turning

to stone. Better to be the stone, to find the end
      of things before it found her. She ripped open

her mother's landscape, roots of hibiscus
      and narcissus like scalps in her fists

 the wound a perfume to Hades, who took her earth
      heavy hands in his. They married by the Styx

where water is free from the weight of reflection.
      In perpetual night she presses his cheek into the sharp bone
         of her hip, breath numbing the ache that stirs

when silver veins of ore glint like sunlight in their chamber.
      Here she can know the hollow without suffering
      echo's fade, taste the fruit's pith

and seed without breaking skin or shade. Here a soul
      can rest, having finally reached its depth.

                    pulp   pulse
In memory   is just another word for
                    pulse   pulp

this sky / my eye

      after Bin Ramke

Sky shaped window
through which
this sky / my eye
reflective dark of
glass reflecting
me inside. My
what a smooth
face a shape
for the gods
who will
awaken sun-
stroked
& darken
what I
should
not
name.

tether / tender

As if the dead wanted

as if earth could unform   empty

                              into itself

decay of dust mites   dynasties

          umbilical cords

planted for luck

          unplucked they tether sediment & sentiment

               birth & after:

gardens plotted at right angles

          geometric souls

that bring us closer

          to gods

Method yields

      to its own making

            Clod that breaks

         Clot that takes

Tongue that tastes

           and tastes

              and tastes

self / shed

When my body forgets
its mind my
hand reaches
toward a face and knows
nothing.

Each winter my skin
chafes

                O snake,

how to leave
a self behind,

let wind take it
as its own

world / ache

ache of inner
ear: sound
of an eggshell heart
as it listens for:

this small chest this small
world breakme break me
open: egg center so solid
a cell I believe in I can
make
            a world

who   can   absolve
the dirt?   pulse   I feel
my   egg   heart   break
      in   silence

we muffle each other:
shellheart   dirtear

                    the old sin-eater has lost his job
                    but I need him still: compact this soil
                    worm after my own heart   cleanse this
                    earth with your wide mouth   sleek body
                    turnip heart you swallow what I cannot

Echomystory
letmehearit
clear
fromthedeepest
mouthseededin
thedarkest

     ground

creature / decreation

bring me into silence with you
I am buried seed
in a forest aflame

that (un)makes I
shout to no one because
all the ears have been stopped / shuttered

by a world that
shudders in flame
stutters in tongues
more tender than rose

the error / of loving / a passing thing

its arrow scribes
my body, my air
that feeds the heat that breaks
me open: world as it uncreates
itself: creature
of its own making

pre- / post-

After our skin sheds
after the sea recedes
after moss turns gray and tongues of birch
peel into silence after
analogy breaks its logic
of a is to b as b is to c
who will wake to a world unmade in our image

Every web gathers, kills, and tears.
I will not rehearse the after, the re-
weaving that makes each day a new pattern
to die upon. The conditions have changed.
Trees no longer bear the weight of filament.
And my limbs are no substitute,
unwilling to wait, unable to still.

warn / warming

we woke up into it
we woke up and it was already burning
I woke up to you telling me so

the mind unhinges in crisis
jaw of a snake

                gentle rabbit, enter
                round rat, come

the logic simple enough, but one we refuse
because we can, because we could
be happier, because an upward curve must peak
eventually and I want to be there when it falls

shake me awake and tell me there are repercussions:
seven minutes for every cigarette I smoke
one mm of sea rise for every plane I take
a child starving for every cake I bake and consume
alone on the tile floor

                hoping you won't come home
                and ask me what I've been

echo / after

Mine is an opening : black breath
also mine
       face full of *coal*
      so close to *foal*
even the way I hold them
both inside my hands

Lump hard : fur soft
old : new
ancient : soon

If sound could save
we'd press fire
into lyre, quake
into wake

Each held
brief
by a body

known only after
by its trace

fossils / making

Carcass me wholly:
shell heart. Caress this
bald spot
here, on my head. Hear
ferns sprout and mountains root.

Here sun edges us
outward, always
pressing our circumference.

A circle is a way of loving
I think   an egg a way
of living inside it.

Think, egg. Can protein clasp your hands
or open them into wings? The *would /should /if*
a luxury, excess of remorse   trace in air.

Breathe it, maybe. Nest that sings for a while
shell that listens for its own breaking.

When the laceration gave way

to marrow

When the nest gave way

to ocean

> the beak left holding the branch
>
> was no longer a miracle

Blubber of otter a record

of our own

> atone this residue with your body
>
> feed on it
>
> and purge
>
> what makes the cell weak inside its shell

dichlorodiphenyLtrichloroethane
dichlorodiphenYltrichloroethane
dichlorodiphenyltRichloroethane
dichlorodipheEnyltrichloroethane
dichlorodiphenyltrIchloroethane
dichlorodiphenylTrichloroethane
dichlorodiphenyltRichloroethane
dichlorodiphenyltrIchloroethane
dichlorodiphEnyltrichloroethane
Dichlorodiphenyltrichloroethane

open a door

the center a threshing, separating you from

airplane, no

bird : machine? Condor etching sun

with wing

watch &
be seen

its body an elegy
in the making
marking &
unmarking
this being

letting me

let me

be

seen

Cast a body into
ocean & watch
as it disappears
then casts
its skull with
corals.   Dump
a few thousand
gallons & watch
them dissipate
then resurface in
gills & wings of
animals both like
& unlike me, next
to but not near
me. Do not ask
the unborn for
absolution. They
can only give you
what   you   leave.

But how can I know my bones from the others?
Bone pile, bone dust. I must stack the fragments
into whole. The test of being is a field
of bones, a bone-white field I walk
across in one line with all the creatures
that ever were flanking all the fields
that ever were. I take whatever is before me:
crushed wing, child's hand, whale's jawbone.
I find each fits, find my new body in the field
of bone, that all the bodies are also my own.

echo / o

Now I can turn

    an urn,

its dark place, this

    face,

beneath its own casing

    Eat.   Sing.

Wind fills the mouth

    in   out

hello?

lo

o

ACKNOWLEDGMENTS

Thank you to the journals and editors who published poems from this collection, often under different titles: *32 Poems, Academy of American Poets, Berkeley Poetry Review, Boston Review, The Cincinnati Review, Colorado Review, The Cresset, CutBank Literary Magazine, Denver Quarterly, Flyway Journal, Grist Journal, Juked, The Laurel Review, The Los Angeles Review, Matter Monthly, Mid-American Review, Ninth Letter, Puerto del Sol, Redivider, Superstition Review, Salamander, TAB: The Journal of Poetry & Poetics, Thrush Poetry Journal, Word Riot, Zone 3*.

My deepest gratitude for everyone who has ever read, listened to, shared, liked, critiqued, questioned, or edited my poems. A special thanks to my mentors and teachers along the way: Paul Willis, who helped shape my early lines into poems; Sasha Steensen, who taught me how to address my poems; Dan Beachy-Quick, who taught me how to listen to them; and Matthew Cooperman, who taught me how to learn the logic of their making. Thank you to Colorado State University, the Lilly Graduate Fellows, and the Vermont Studio Center for supporting this project at different stages across the years, as well as to the incredible peers and mentors I learned from there. Thank you to Carrie Olivia Adams, Janaka Stucky, Nikkita Cohoon, and the whole Black Ocean crew for believing in my work and treating it with such care. Thank you to my family, friends, and fellow travelers for your enduring generosity and belief in my work. And thank you, Levi, for staying in the making with me.